⊱⊶⊱⊶⊱⊶⊱⊶

NOT
REMEMBERED
NEVER
FORGOTTEN

⊱⊶⊱⊶⊱⊶⊱⊶

NOT REMEMBERED NEVER FORGOTTEN

An Adoptee's Search for His Birthfamily

❖❖❖❖❖

A true story by
Robert Allan Hafetz

GATEWAY PRESS, INC.
Baltimore, MD   2005

Please direct all correspondence and book orders to:
Robert Allan Hafetz
1014 Surrey Lane
Warrington, PA 18976

Library of Congress Control Number 2005929042
ISBN 0-9770202-0-7

Published for the author by
Gateway Press, Inc.
3600 Clipper Mill Rd., Suite 260
Baltimore, MD 21211-1953

www.gatewaypress.com

Printed in the United States of America

Acknowledgement
My warmest gratitude to my wife,
Arleen, who endured the year of my
search and then volunteered to be
my editor.

" A musician must make music, an artist must paint, a poet must write, if he is to be at peace with himself.

What a man can be, he must be. This is the need we may call self-actualization...

It refers to man's desire for fulfillment, namely to the tendency for him to become actually what he is potentially: to become everything that one is capable of becoming."

Abraham Maslow

Table of Contents

Illustrations

Why I Wrote This Book

I have two objectives in writing this account of my adoption experience; the first is to help all members of the adoption family in dealing with their loss, a loss that society does not recognize. The child, the natural mother and the adopted family all experience profound loss. The adoptive parents have a need to overcome their inability to have a child of their own and this will affect the way they interact with their adopted child. My adopted mother always feared the existence of my natural mother so it was never discussed. I was told I was adopted as a child, but we never explored how I felt about it. Throughout our lives together, my mother would offer me the opportunity to ask her about anything. Often, I always brought up my adoption and asked what she knew about my natural mother. Always, she refused to answer or even acknowledge the question, looking away and then changing the subject. My adopted mother held on to this fear to the last day of her life. I believe it would have drawn us closer together if we had explored our feelings about this.

The second and more elusive challenge is to explain to those of you who are not members of the adoption family what that special loss is like. I have tried many times to share my loss and grief with my wife, but I can tell by the expression on her face that she doesn't grasp the depth and intensity of the grief of adoption. Like society, she believes that adoption is an act of selfless love by the natural mother and generous love by the adoptive parents. The adopted child has a second chance, a new complete family, love, attention, literally a new life.

One pictures the smiling baby held by his adopted mother, hugged, nurtured, cherished and kept safe from harm. My adopted family loved me as their own. I couldn't have asked for better parents. What more could a human being ever want? Their love and affection sustains me, and gives me what I need to grow and survive but it doesn't replace what has been lost. I want what others have; a name given at birth, a heritage, and a memory of my mother's face.

Think back as far as you can and try to recall your earliest memory. It's almost impossible to remember anything before the age of four, but the memories are there. Psychology teaches us that we lose the ability to recall those memories, but they are in our minds. There's a good chance that the oldest memories you were able to recall were powerful events, even traumatic. These are the memories that stay with us the longest, and the more powerful the event, the stronger the ability to recall that memory. We recall those memories in complex pictures and words, but what if a memory occurred before we could speak, or before our minds were mature? That memory would exist in the form of a feeling rather than in pictures or words. Now imagine that you're a baby, and in those early moments of life you are held by your mother. A mother you have been a part of for the past nine months. Imagine that you see your mother's face, hear her voice calling your name, speaking softly to you. You smell her, feel her, and hear the sound of her heart beating against your body....... Then suddenly she's gone!

You grow up with a feeling that you can't express in words or even in pictures because when it happened you couldn't speak. How then do you tell someone about it when you don't understand it yourself? You can't picture it, your mind wasn't developed when it happened; you can't describe it, even to yourself. All you have is a sense of loss, profound loss. So like many adopted children you bury it and go on with life. Some of us will keep the memory buried forever, but for many of us we are compelled to resolve it. It was believed that a newborn couldn't have such memories of separation and that it was the adult mother who had to cope with her guilt. It was believed that the mother would get over the trauma and the child wouldn't have to. That belief was wrong on both counts.

The most effective word I can use to describe the emotion I'm discussing is grief. It is grief that both mother and child feel resulting from the separation. When humans feel grief, we support them so that they can travel through a grieving process and resolve their intense emotions. Grief is what we associate with death, but grief can result from other severed relationships as well. That's why we have funerals, divorces, and going away rituals. We even grieve for temporary separations in a less intense way because we recognize the human pain of separation. What grief

4

process is there for the adopted child who suffers the greatest of all separations? Our need is denied, and even disbelieved. They will ask what could a baby possibly know from an event occurring at such a young age, but the truth is we know.

Adopted children and adults can easily be trapped in the early stages of grief. Since the loss occurs in infancy, before one has the ability to speak, adoptees experience a unique difficulty in examining their emotions. Lacking words and conscious memories of our loss, we cannot express our grief to loved ones. The state of being unable to understand and express what we feel prevents us from moving forward and resolving our grief.

Grief does not diminish over time. It waits for the moment when it can come to the surface. It speaks, not in the language of words, but in the feelings of emotions. It never tires and it never gives up. When trying to understand what many adopted adults are emotionally experiencing, think of the loss of a loved one. Human relationships don't end when people are separated by death, distance, or time.

The Author age 8

Part One

Not Remembered, Never Forgotten

"Youth in April
A young woman and man,
Share a moment together,
And then
I am."

I am Robert, but I once had another name. As an infant I was held and loved by two women, one who would give me up, and another who raised me and loved me more than life itself. I suppose I should consider myself blessed to have been loved by two mothers when most of us get only one, and some none. My adopted father was a physician, a gentle man who devoted his life to helping the helpless. One didn't need an appointment to see him; patients just came to his office and waited. He would come home when his waiting room was empty. My mother was a Jewish immigrant from Poland, having escaped the wave of Nazism that swept across Europe. She left all that she knew and came to America with her brother and sisters. I am today the essence of my adopted father's caring humanity and my adopted mother's courage and relentless strength. Let me end all doubt that being raised in a bad home makes the adoptee search; it has nothing to do with it. My home was a blessing.

I came upon the world on January 28, 1951, somewhere in Jersey City, New Jersey. That was what my amended birth certificate stated. Adoptees never see their actual birth certificate; they only see a fictitious one and there is no way to know if the amended one is true or false. My parents believed I should know I was a "chosen" child and consequently, my awareness of being adopted is one of my earliest memories. I was told few facts about my birth mother; she was Jewish, single, and the agency was the Jewish Family Service. This is all I ever knew about my actual history. I assumed my adoptive family's heritage as my own and wore it like an ill fitting coat, keeping me warm in winter and the rain off my back, but I always knew it wasn't really mine. From my earliest memories I always had a strong drive to discover my past, to know who I would have been, and what kind of people created me. I yearned to know if I had brothers and sisters. I wanted, more than anything to see a face that resembled my own. Soon, the truth was about to be revealed to me, and I would discover exactly why I had such strong feelings about a mother I never knew.

Every adopted child must, eventually, wonder about the events that caused their adoption. Was I given up out of an act of selfless love or, abandoned, because I was a problem that needed a quick solution? Searching involves the risk that the truth might be painful, and many adoptees refuse to search because what they might discover could be devastating. This was one of two reasons why I delayed beginning my search. The second was my belief that my adopted mother would be hurt by my need to know who my birth mother was. My adopted mother was always reluctant to discuss the events surrounding my adoption. I later discovered the reason for this reluctance, the reason that she had great fear that my birth mother would come back for me.

My life has always been filled with unanswered questions that seemed to have a life of their own, always there, just under the surface, lurking, and waiting for an opportunity to come out and demand an answer. On holidays, I always wondered what my birthmother and possible siblings were doing at that moment. I assumed in my child's mind, that when I was celebrating a holiday, they were as well, and in that moment we were together. I was making a desperate connection to reach across the void that separated us. Did my natural mother wonder what the son she gave away was doing? On my birthday I was certain my mother was thinking of me as I was thinking of her, possibly at that very same point in time. I felt comfort in that thought, because in that moment, I believed, we were connected by our thoughts and feelings. This was the closest I could ever be to her for most of my life.

I will assert that after all my searching, I have discovered two unique characteristics, possibly divine in nature, that characterize us as human beings. The first is altruism, without which I could not have succeeded in my search. All along the way I encountered people who offered their help with no benefit to themselves. Adoption case workers, after they told me that I wasn't in their files, still wouldn't let me end the conversation and asked me many questions so they could direct my search. Strangers who met with me and shared their high school year books and memories, brought their friends with them, walked through cemeteries in the winter cold, looking for a gravestone that might give me a clue, and a seventy-seven year-old Cantor in Florida who offered to do whatever it took, and found a crucial piece of this great puzzle. The second virtue is the bond between a mother and her child. It is the strongest bond in all of humanity, reaching across decades, miles, and even life itself, to touch, nurture, and shape the character of her child. Once a mother bonds with her new-born, a connection is created that cannot be broken. It thrives and grows, it compels and nurtures, it does not weaken with time, but in fact grows stronger, drawing them together again at some point in time. The infant, even though not developed, unable to speak, and with only the most basic ability to perceive the world, knows his mother's face, her voice, and her touch. The child grows into adulthood and cannot consciously remember those events, but they are there, never forgotten. Not remembered and never forgotten are the thoughts and feelings that bond mother and child separated in infancy. How can something so compelling and powerful be so concealed? There must be something divine in the creation of this relationship.

The answers to all my questions sat in a locked file in the Surrogate Court in the state of New Jersey. The state does not recognize my need to know who my birth family is. In fact, they are legally obligated to keep me from finding my mother. I don't have a birth certificate; they made one up and called it amended. Then they locked the truth away forever. The objective of this confidentiality is to protect the birth mother from the social stigma of an out of wedlock birth. The adoptive family is also protected from the birth mother or her family intruding into the child's life and possibly disrupting the developmental process. However, after the child has reached adulthood, the confidentiality only serves as a barrier to the reuniting of birth family and child. The law, in its concreteness, doesn't address this need and assumes that the social dynamics remain the same for a developing child and a grown adult. To paraphrase Locke, *An adult, as a citizen, owns a property, in his own person.* I demand from the state the deed to my person. I demand the right that I have been endowed with at birth, to know who I am, to be respected by the state, just like everyone else.

Dr. and Mrs. Florence Hafetz
My adoptive parents

Week One

The Search

A trail 52 years old is a very cold one

I began the search on a quiet winter day, shortly after my 52nd birthday. My adoptive parents were deceased, my father for sixteen years and my mother for two years. I could never bring myself to search while my adoptive mother was alive as I believed, correctly, that she would be hurt. I waited until she passed away and my grief resolved, to begin; realizing later, that I had let slip away the best source of information I had. However, I could not begin the search unless I was comfortable in my heart that it was the right thing to do and in the right way.

I gathered what little information I had, my amended birth certificate, and the only two facts my adopted mother ever mentioned; my name was originally Marvin and the agency was Jewish Family and Children's Service. I met with an attorney recommended by a close friend. The attorney was generous enough to spend an hour with me at no cost. He gave me a number of adoption support groups, addresses and websites, and briefed me on how little legal standing I had to petition the New Jersey Superior Court. Even if I had a medical need to know about my family's history, they would only give me medical information with no names. Unknown to me at the time was that the lack of knowledge of my family's medical history almost would cost me my life. I have cardio vascular disease that started at a very young age and by the time I was in my early 40s, I had three blocked arteries that brought me to within a hair's breath of a massive heart attack. It never happened because my healthy lifestyle consisting of frequent and vigorous exercise had created a condition called angiogenesis, commonly known as a natural by-pass. However, I required an angioplasty to correct the blocked arteries. Had I known I had this genetic predisposition, I would have been tested early in my life for the risk factors. The lawyer and I decided that I should concentrate my search on finding the adoption agency that arranged my adoption and that if I needed to go to court, he would be willing to represent me.

Week Two

The Internet

This is the age of information processing and at my disposal is the vast body of data called the internet. Using the Net, I searched for Jewish Family and Children's Service agencies in the Jersey City area where I was born. It really seemed simple, perhaps too simple, all I had to do was find the agency, contact them, and they would contact my birth family or so I thought. Searches produced phone numbers and each call always produced the same response, "We didn't have anything to do with your adoption." In all fairness, the case workers always referred me to another agency that they believed could help me, but the response was always the same. There was no central data bank and every agency had its own separate filing system. Getting information over fifty years old was difficult; it was usually buried or long ago discarded. I was hitting a wall with every phone call and I was starting to feel frustrated. After many intense hours, the only thing I had accomplished was a list of adoption agencies that didn't conduct my adoption.

I have listed my name on many adoption registries, but without a birth name or any other knowledge of my family I don't hold much hope for this to bear fruit. The only piece of information that I have in common with my birthmother is my date of birth, assuming it's real and has not been created for my false birth certificate. I am hoping there is a remote chance that if anyone is looking for me, then my birthday will be the key that attracts their attention. Here, in the age of information processing, I am doing the equivalent of writing a note and putting it in a bottle.

Week Three

A canyon and no bridge

More phone calls and more dead ends; the cycle of hope and frustration continues. For long periods of time I just sit in front of the computer, overcome with sorrow. This isn't like me; I have always been steadfast in the face of adversity, always willing to find hope and push on. Adversity has never defeated me, but has only made me stronger. This time it was different; this time the stakes were very high. I did a lot of soul searching, and realized that I had released emotions that I had kept hidden all my life. Very powerful emotions whose intensity I couldn't understand. Why is this search as important as it feels? This has become the most important event in my life and I am devoting more time and energy to it than to my work. I am a recreation therapist at a mental hospital for emotionally disturbed adolescents. Many are foster children and I care very much about them, but this search has taken on a life of its own and I don't know where it's coming from. My wife tells me I look terrible and that I should stop for awhile. I can see in her face she doesn't understand why this is so important to me. I am at a loss myself at times to understand why I have such an all encompassing need to know about a person of whom I have never been consciously aware. I know that I have no memory of my mother's face, her voice, her touch and that I don't know anything about her. I would later discover that I was wrong. It is true that I could not remember, but it was also true that I could not forget. I am afraid of what I will learn.

Week Four

Friendship is a bridge across the widest chasm

I don't always understand how or why things happen, but I have learned to accept truth when it comes from a source not anticipated or understood. As an adopted only child with no siblings, I learned to make friendships that took the place of brothers and sisters that I never had. Friends were the same as family to me and I held on to my friends. I created relationships that lasted for as long as I can remember. Sometimes a little help from your friends can pull you through the worst of times. Two years ago I rediscovered my ninth grade girlfriend, Linda Abrams, now an accomplished doctor of psychology in her own private practice. She offered me inspiration and guidance in my search, doing what she could to help me. She invested herself into helping me and provided me an abundance of advice, inspiration, and direction. I turned to my old friend and explained to her that I had called every Jewish Family and Children's Service adoption agency in New Jersey, New York and Pennsylvania, with the same lack of success, leaving me at a dead end. She said, "Why don't you go see a psychic?" I must admit that this is something I never would have considered on my own and I was very skeptical when my friend mentioned it. Considering the amount of my success during the past month, I couldn't do any worse. If anyone else had suggested this I would have laughed it off, but Linda was serious and her investment in my search was beyond question. I asked her to suggest one and in short order I had a name and an appointment.

Week Five

Crossing over, here goes nothing

I can't believe that I am doing this, but here I sit in the home of Carol London, a psychic reader. I have no idea of what to expect and I am determined to keep an open mind. Since I have so few facts and I am looking for some very specific information, it will be easy to determine if the session will be a success. It will either give me direction or it will not. It will either help or it will not help. My questions are concrete and categorical, where is the adoption agency, where is my birth family, what can you tell me about the events of my birth and adoption?

The session begins with Ms. London and I seated on her sofa, in her home in Elkins Park, PA. She asks me if she should withhold any information that might be upsetting to me, to which I reply, "No, I want to know everything." I give her the only information I know, I was born in Jersey City, New Jersey on Jan 28, 1951 and Jewish Family and Children's Service was the agency. Carol looks away for a moment, as if to collect her thoughts, and then she speaks to me. "Your mother is thin, very thin, she has green eyes and dark hair. Her pregnancy is known to her family, you were 6 LBS at birth, your father was in the Army, traveled, and never knew you were born or that your mother was pregnant. I see a red cradle or rocking chair, and you should search in Cape May, New Jersey. Look for a place called Lutheran Ministries Adoption. In its name is a red cradle. You were not born in a hospital; you were born in a place with a red shield. I see the seashore and you have something to do with the ocean. You were wanted and loved by your birth family." Ms. London also spoke of my adopted family and stated that my father had a terrible cough at his death. She then said he felt like he drowned when he died. That really got my attention because my father was on a breathing tube and he pulled it out of his throat causing a cough. He couldn't speak to me in the last moments of his life because of that cough. He died of congestive heart failure, the equivalent of drowning, caused by fluid draining into the lungs, and only two people alive were aware of that; my wife and myself. I began to take Ms. London seriously, but the information she gave me didn't really make any sense. Red cradles and shields, Cape May, Lutheran Ministries; I was Jewish for heavens sake, where is all this coming from?

The next morning I sit once again at my computer, with new information that makes no sense whatsoever. It's as if I was given a puzzle with the pieces scattered all around and little idea of what the picture should look like. The last thing Carol said was look for Lutheran Ministries Adoptions in Cape May, so that's what I put into my search engine. As the screen began to form, I could see that the picture was mostly red; a representation of the state of New Jersey appeared. If you used your imagination, you could say that the state looks like a red cradle on its side or even a rocking chair. Encouraged, I contacted them and they said they would research it and that I should call them back. Three hours later I called them and the intake worker recognized me from my request. She told me that this agency didn't handle my adoption. Failure once again, and, in all honesty, what could I really expect from a session with a psychic?

Like so many kind hearted people, the intake worker said, "Wait, don't hang up, maybe I can help you. Tell me, where, were you were adopted?" I tell her what little I know, that I was born in Jersey City and raised in Trenton. She says, "When you were adopted fifty-two years ago, there were not many adoption agencies and only two that handled adoptions in the Trenton area. Since you were raised in Trenton, you should look there for the agency." She gave me two phone numbers and said good luck. I called the first number and that was the Children's Home Society of New Jersey. Once again the case worker said she would look in the records and call me back if she found anything. I felt it was time to stop and take a rest for awhile. I'm emotionally tired, and worn out, and I really don't know what to do at this point anyway.

The phone rings and a caseworker named Marie is on the line. "Is this Bob?" she asks. I say, "Yes", and she says, "I can help you." I can't speak. I'm not prepared to hear what I wanted so desperately to hear to hear, and she repeats her statement; "I can help you." I am unable to speak and she says, "If you can fax me some identification, I will mail you some information." Recovering my composure, I ask, "What time do you open tomorrow morning?" Now the journey begins.

It is 9:00 the next morning and accompanied by my wife, I am sitting in the office of Marie Braun at the Children's Home Society of Trenton. I am 5 city blocks from my adopted father's place of business, and 5 miles from the home where I was raised. After looking across three states for the agency, I find myself back home once again. Marie sits smiling at us from across her metal desk; in front of her sits a manila folder with the answers to the most important questions I have ever asked. I am tempted to grab the file and run out of the office, but the feeling dissolves as she begins to speak. She tells me that many of their adopted children return and I am not alone in my search. It is her job to bring me in and help me deal with the issues that I will be facing. She states that she can only give me non identifying information and then she reads to me from the folder. "Your mother had green eyes and dark brown hair, she was 5'4" tall and weighed 110 LBS, your father was in the army and never knew you were born, you were 6LBS 13 OZS.

Your mother didn't want to give you up and her family considered adopting you themselves. After you were born, you lived in a foster home and your mother visited you often." I was stunned; Carol London had spoken almost those very same words to me two days ago. Then I asked Marie about the red shield and where I was born. She showed me a symbol that I recognized immediately, the Salvation Army Shield. I was born at a Booth Home called the Door of Hope in Jersey City, New Jersey. That's the red shield, the symbol of the Salvation Army. The pieces of the puzzle given to me by Carol London are starting to come together. A mother who didn't want to give me up, grandparents who considered adopting me, and for the first five months of my life my mother held me, spoke to me, called my name and I heard her name, saw her face and felt her touch. I will never remember those moments, but I will never forget them. This bond between a mother and her child is not remembered, but never forgotten. It lives in my mind, playing a role in my life as a presence that can't be seen, but that asserts itself, guides me and nurtures me in ways I will soon discover. Slowly I began to understand these feelings I have always had. I was not a newborn taken from his mother; I was a five-month-old, bonded child, separated from his mother. At some level of awareness, I knew what happened to me. I know I will find her no matter what it takes or how long.

The Children's Home Society Search

Committed but not aggressive

I am delivered into the hands of a social worker whose full time job is to search for birth families. She conducts an assessment to evaluate my state of mind and to prepare me for the possibility that the outcome may not be as I expect it to be. My mother may refuse to accept a meeting, be in denial, mentally ill, shocked at my return, or she may be deceased. Her family may regard me as an outsider, with shock, suspicion and contempt. I could be rejected and abandoned again, a thought too terrible to confront. My only guide is my own heart, and I ask myself what I would want if it were my child. I have no doubt that I would want to be together again, to make right what was made wrong. I am taking a great risk, not only to my life, but to the lives of the family I have never known. I am intruding into their lives? Will I be a painful memory long forgotten, or a virtual stranger? Who am I to invade their homes and family, to disturb the order of their lives? I am my mother's first natural born son, connected to them, in my flesh and in my heart and soul. I am a part of them and they are a part of me. During the time I ponder this difficult question, I feel the pull of my natural mother, the not forgotten connection, drawing me closer and compelling me to go forward. I know in my heart that to go forward is right and I will accept the outcomes no matter what they might be. I feel like I am being guided, and urged to continue. With each barrier comes new hope and inspiration. I do something I have never before in my life done, I pray often. I am certain and clear as I instruct the social worker to begin the search.

I Wait

and wait, and wait, and wait

The weeks go by and I am given reports by the social worker that they are experiencing some difficulty finding my natural mother's family. Their approach is to find an obituary for one of her parents and from that, a living relative. They can find no obituaries. I start to search on my own again, while they search and possibly we could pool our resources. This is made difficult by their refusal to give me any identifying data, but I now have a history of my families. The following narrative was given to me by the social worker; it was the story of my life as told to me for the first time.

COMPLETE BACKGROUND REPORT
ROBERT HAFETZ

You were born on January 28, 1951 at 12:08 PM in Jersey City, New Jersey. You weighed 6 pounds 11 ounces and were 21 ½ inches long. After leaving the hospital, you remained in a Children's Home Society foster home until joining your adoptive family on June 15, 1951.

Your birth mother was 17 years old at the time of your birth. She was single, of the Jewish faith, of German and Russian descent. Your birth mother's social worker at that time found her to be quite refined and intelligent. She was described as being attractive with brown hair and green eyes. She was 5' 4" tall and weighed 110 pounds. She was in her senior year of high school and taking college prep courses. During the summers, she worked in a hotel office. She hoped to go on to college. She had no other children at the time of your birth and adoption. Your birth mother had one older brother. He died at age seven of meningitis when your birth mother was only three months old. There is no other information about him in the record.

Your birth mother's mother, your maternal grandmother was 43 years old at the time of your birth and adoption. She had black hair and brown eyes. She was 5' 4" tall with an average build. She was a high school graduate and employed as the manager of a hotel. She came down with tuberculosis six months after the death of her son. She felt it was due to her being so upset about his death. Other than this, she was reported as being in good health. Your maternal grandmother had one sister who was 45 years old at that time. She too had black hair, brown eyes, was 5' 4" tall and was a high school graduate. Your maternal grandmother's mother, your great grandmother, was 68 years old at the time of your birth. She was said to look just like your birth mother. She had black hair, brown eyes, with a short average build. She was educated in Europe and came to the United States from Austria at the age of 16. She was in good health, although she had arthritis. Your maternal great grandfather was born in this country. He was 5'6" tall with a slender build and brown eyes and hair. He had an eighth grade education and worked as a special policeman. He had been in good health, but 5 years before you were born, he began suffering from a bad heart.

Your birth mother's father, your maternal grandfather was 45 years old at the time of your birth.

He had brown hair, green eyes, was 5' 10" tall with a slender build. He was a high school graduate and managed a hotel with his wife. He was a chef and supervised the kitchen. Your maternal grandfather had four brothers and three sisters. All were in good health with brown eyes and hair. Two sisters and one brother were high school graduates. The others had public school educations. Their occupations were butcher, salesman, and saleslady. All were married with the exception of one sister. Your maternal grandfather's mother died at the age of 42 of the flu. She was born in Russia. Your maternal grandfather's father died at the age of 52 from pneumonia. He too was born in Russia. He was a hatter and was in good health.

The Birthfather

Your birth father was 21 years old at the time of your birth. He was single, of the Protestant religion and Welsh decent. He had blonde wavy hair and green eyes. He was 5'6" tall with a medium build. He left school in his junior year to take a job as a mechanic.

At the time of your birth he was in the army. He was in good health.

Your birth father had four brothers and two sisters. All were of average height and build with green eyes and blond hair. The youngest was thirteen years old at the time of your birth and the oldest was thirty. They all graduated from high school with the exception of the youngest. All but the two youngest were married. The brothers bought a garage together and were mechanics.

Your birth father's mother, your paternal grandmother was 50 years old at the time of your birth. She was 5'6" tall with a heavyset build. She had blonde hair and green eyes. She did not graduate from high school and was never employed outside of the home. She had a bad heart.

Your birth father's father, your paternal grandfather, was in his late fifties at the time of your birth. He was 5' 6" tall with a thin build, light brown hair and green eyes. He was a coal minor with little education. He was working in a parking lot at the time of your birth.

Your birth parents met while in high school and knew each other for a period of three years. Your birth mother described him as being very handsome and felt she was in love with him. She later learned that this had been an infatuation. Your birth mother did not know your birth father's whereabouts when she discovered her pregnancy. She knew that marriage to him was not an option for her. She also believed that she was not ready for marriage and was ready to go to college. Your birth mother visited you and had difficulty releasing you for adoption; she believed that your adoption into a stable loving two parent family was in your best interest.

Even without names there is an abundance of information contained in this non-identifying history. It provides me with my families' religion, occupation, ages at the time of my birth, physical descriptions, but is there enough information contained in this narrative to enable me to find a record of my grandparents? Three days ago I was frustrated, exhausted and hopeless, now today I have hope and direction.

My Search Begins in Earnest

"Hope is a rose in autumn
A ladybug on a leaf
Symbols out of time
help me,
with my grief"

Hope is what sustains us when there is an absence of facts. When we have a compelling need, and lack the information to direct us to the fulfillment of that need, we depend on hope to support us. Hope can therefore be defined as the belief that a goal is attainable in spite of evidence that it is not. It's unreasonable and illogical, but it's another defining quality of what it means to be human. To be without it, to be in a state of hopelessness, is a condition that we all want to avoid and we understand this concept without argument. Clinically, the persistent state of hopelessness is called depression. We even consider it, objectively, to be a disorder requiring treatment. There were many times when I had no more options, when every avenue I tried ended in failure. To embark on a task that results in one failure after another and to persist in that task may appear to an observer as deranged behavior. It debilitates the mind and body and tears down the soul, but always there is a spark of hope. When I face a wall in my search I return to nature. I walk in the woods, or sit in my garden. I think about the flowers and I think about God. The state of being alone has always held great fear for me and I have learned to pray to drive away that fear. Prayers I said often as a child have taken on a new meaning, or perhaps it's me that has learned to understand what was always there. Prayers must have been inspired by times of great human need and when we are in need their meaning becomes self evident.

I collect all the information I have and try and create a geographic picture of where my natural family lived and worked. I know that I was born in Jersey City, that my grandparents managed a hotel, and that my birth father was of Welsh descent. I take a map of New Jersey and starting from Jersey City, I look for resort areas that existed in the 1940s and '50s. Starting from The Atlantic Highlands, I work my way south along the coast to Atlantic City. The Internet is a marvelous tool as every city has its own website with a complete history and its achievements. The problem is that there are so many of them and most of the grand old hotels are long gone. I learn about an era of elegance and happiness at the Jersey shore; a hotel industry that drew people from all over the United States and Canada. This was the place to vacation. As a child, my adopted parents took me to Atlantic City, Lakewood and Asbury Park, and I remember those times with much happiness. I remember names of hotels like The Laurel in the Pines in Lakewood, and the Traymore Hotel in Atlantic City. I discover that the Traymore was knocked down to make room for a casino and the Laural in the Pines burned in a terrible fire. Most of this grand and elegant history is gone forever, saved only in the minds of those who remember, and some authors who felt the need to preserve the grandeur of the Jersey Shore.

In my searching, I discover that the Atlantic Highlands was settled in the early 20th century by immigrants from Wales. This gives me a reference point and I focus my search in the area surrounding the Highlands. There are many small towns and they are all very much alike. I use classmates.com to find lists of people who would have graduated in 1951 or '52. I wrote to hundreds of them and ask them if they knew a young Jewish girl, with an older boyfriend, who suddenly dropped out of sight in the middle of her senior year. I was hoping that small town gossip would have revealed a forbidden romance like the one my mother claimed she had. Many people responded with encouragement and kindness, but none knew of this couple. Once again I am facing a dead end. I decide to see Carol London once again.

The Second Session

Not north and Not south

Carol London and I have become close friends as she has taken a personal interest in my search. I believe she has a special gift that rises from her empathy and intuition. It's important to explain that the information she gives me must be examined from every possible perspective. It isn't always clear and often its meaning is hidden in pictures and phrases I don't understand, but become clear as I get closer to the truth. She has put me in the right direction before and I wouldn't have come this far without her. What I am hoping for is a clue, something that will narrow my search. Once again we sit together on her couch and once again the session is in the form of a casual conversation. I give her the background report to read and after she reads it she speaks. It appears to me that she hears information and must then interpret it and relate it to me. It's like whisper down the lane, only the lane is my history. Sometimes she will tell me things that aren't clear and at times she speaks with absolute certainty. She says, "Your family lived in the place where they worked." "It's not Atlantic City, it was not south and it was not north. There was an inland body of water, like a small river, a large government complex, a warehouse, and a high school with four stories." She also said my grandparents lived in the hotel. I question her about Atlantic City and she is adamant telling me no, it's a part of New Jersey that's not north and not south. When Carol is certain about something she lets you know it. She's talking loudly, as if she is frustrated that I don't understand. Not north and not south, where can that be?

I am back to the Internet and I trace the coastal towns from Sandy Hook to Atlantic City. Not north and not south must be central New Jersey along the coast. I am able to find each city's website and I look for a picture of a high school with four stories. It's not easy to find. The pictures are of new schools and the one I want is half a century old. I do find a place with an auto repair shop called Brothers Auto and I remember that from the background report of my birth father. It's in a place called Keyport and I decide to travel there and see for myself. My wife and I take the Garden State Parkway up to Keyport, New Jersey. We park and walk around. It's a beautiful coastal town, but within minutes I know in my heart that this is not the place. I have been told by other adoptees that when they found their home town, they knew the minute they set foot there that it was the right place.

It's time to take another look at my information and I see less than ten possible cities and shore towns. I reflect on my thoughts for the umpteenth time with my patient wife who has heard me thinking out loud for the past four months. I have a habit of talking to empty space while she is in the room and she always assumes I'm speaking to her. "Where would a Jewish married couple be employed as hotel managers at the Jersey shore?" It can't be too far north or too far south." A voice from out of thin air interrupts my thoughts, "Asbury Park," she says," My parents always took me to Asbury Park when I was a child," my wife insists. Years of marriage have taught her how to change the tone of her voice to cut through the haze of male single mindedness. I immediately go to the computer and bring up a map of New Jersey and there it is, a shore resort area, in central New Jersey along the shore. It was also the center of Jewish culture in the 1940s and supported a large Jewish community. I find a website for Asbury Park and I can see a picture of the high school. It has three stories. I also see the Naval Ammunition Depot a few miles north, it's a large warehouse, and an inlet, like a river, runs through the city. I will focus my search on Asbury Park.

Asbury Park

One must read between the lines
to find the truth

The social worker reports to me that she has discovered some information. She has discovered the death notice of my grandmother. She will only tell me that my grandmother died in Florida in 1990. Three weeks later they discover the death notice for my grandfather; he also died in Florida, in 1996. There were no obituaries that they could find and they wouldn't tell me what city. I ask the social worker a carefully phrased question; " I am investing a great deal of time and emotional energy searching in the Asbury Park area, can you please tell me that this is not the place where my family lived." She replied "I cannot discuss the place where your parents lived and worked." Is she trying to tell me something? She could have simply said no comment or I can't discuss it. I believe there was a clear message in her reply. I believe that Asbury Park is in fact the place where my family lived and worked. I drive to Asbury Park and stand before the high school. When I first looked at it I thought it had three stories, but as I looked more closely I saw there was a fourth floor cafeteria. I hadn't noticed it before the first time I looked. A high school with four stories; this was the school Carol London spoke of. I don't have any real proof that this is the right place, but I have hope that it is, even stronger; I believe that it is.

I walk through the neighborhoods surrounding the school. It's a place with two distinct characters. The hotels, amusement park, and boardwalks, are all gone. The elegance and charm of this 1950s resort city lives on only as a memory in the minds of the adults who experienced the joys of childhood here. Today empty rundown buildings and fields of concrete are all that remain of this once thriving center of leisure. The neighborhoods are quiet, intimate, and unchanged since my birth. It's a place where neighbors know each other and look out for each other. The wide streets are covered with tall mature trees, their roots breaking through the sidewalks. The houses have front porches, slate roofs, and everything is a short walk away. Near the ocean, Victorian houses with large wraparound porches stand today as they did fifty-five years ago. The salty breeze drifting in from the ocean fills my senses. I reflect on how far I have come with so little to start with. I may have found my birth families' home town. Somewhere in this place is the story of the beginning of my life and the history of my family. This is a good place, it feels like home.

I make the two hour drive to Asbury Park many times during the next month. I spend hours in the library researching city directories. Before there were phone books or yellow pages people used city directories to organize information. Residents were listed by phone number, and street address. The members of the family were listed and the employment of the head of the household was stated as well. I was hoping to find a husband and wife who managed a hotel but without a name it or any specific information I would have to stumble on them by chance. I looked at the business section under hotels but there were so many of them. Hotels with names like; The Albion, The Metropolitan, The Plaza, and The Ambassador. Places from another age of grace and elegance now they are empty shells or dust with no one there to speak to me and give up their secrets.

Adoption Forum

Before you can succeed
You must believe you can succeed

Once again confronted by dead ends and despair, I decided to seek help through an adoption support group. I joined Adoption Forum which offered me a local monthly support group. The group reflected all points of the adoption triad; I met a birth mother who searched for her son, an adoptee who searched for her mother, and a mother who adopted. They were sensitive, supporting, and understood the emotions I was feeling. It's always easier to explain what one feels to those who have experienced a similar loss. I brought all my files and folders and showed them the information that I had compiled. I was surprised by the force of their interest and the commitment they displayed. One member suggested I use the Social Security Death Index. The Social Security Administration maintains a database recording all deaths of anyone who received benefits. Their interest was contagious, and from their determination alone, I developed a new sense of hope. I can't remember how many times I went through the cycle of hope and despair only to be revived by the kindness of a stranger. The sense of commitment I felt from these people who share the same adoption experience was very powerful and comforting. As a result of this, I believe that every adopted child is the "sibling of circumstance" of every other adopted child. We who share the same thoughts and desires, ask the same questions, and search for the same answers to our common spiritual need, have become a family in our own right. "Siblings of circumstance," bound by the emptiness and the desire to end it.

After carefully reviewing my files and asking me a lot of questions one of the members proclaimed, "You have enough information to find your grandparents; it can be done with what you have, I'm sure of it." I had no idea how, but I left the meeting that night with the firm belief that it can be done and that I would find the names of my grandparents. Before you can succeed you must believe you can succeed.

Something From Nothing

I have become an Alchemist

I have discovered the Social Security Death Index on the internet. It is a free database, consisting of all the people who ever collected Social Security and passed away. I know that somewhere in that database are the names of my grandparents, but how do I find them. If this isn't the proverbial needle in a haystack, then I don't know what is. I keep hearing in my mind the words of my fellow adoptee, "It can be done." I arrange the information I have so that it's on my desk right in front of me. I know their age at my birth, so I can estimate their year of birth, and the state in which they originally started working. The adoption agency told me their age at death, and that they died in Florida. The question before me is, do I have enough information to do a query and isolate a small enough number of names from the Social Security database? My grandfather passed away at the age of nintey and most men don't live that long, consequently, I believe I have a good chance of generating a manageable list of names. I begin with him, and using the advanced search engine, I enter my data, age at death ninety, year of birth 1905, last residence Florida, benefits issued in New Jersey, then hit enter. I am now looking at a list of eight hundred thirty-four names and one of them has to be my grandfather's. I remove all the females, and now I am down to less than three hundred names. I know my grandfather was Jewish, of Russian decent, so I remove as many Smiths, Robinsons, and any other names that are clearly not ethnically related. I am left with thirty-two names. One of these names has to be it, but which one? I can't call them or write to them. The computer age is a miracle of information processing, but I still can't send an E mail to Heaven. I forge ahead and repeat the process with a focus on my grandmother. I have now a list of over thirteen hundred women and a list of thirty-two men. The haystack is somewhat smaller, but it's still a haystack nonetheless. There has to be a way to figure this out because it can be done. I have an inspiration, I am looking for a husband and a wife, and therefore they must have the same last name. What if I took the names from the men and inserted it into the search engine with all the data from the initial search I did for my grandmother. I would find a woman with the same last name and I would only have to do thirty-two searches. When two names matched, there was a good chance they would be husband and wife and therefore my grandparents. I did it and it worked, I had two sets of names that matched and their city of death was also the same.

Time stops for me as it dawns on me that I may have discovered my birth name. There is an eerie quiet that accompanies such a moment, an inner stillness as if the world is in one place and I am in another, but there is still a shadow of doubt.

The first matching names I explore are Koplowitz. They are of Russian Jewish ancestry, are the right age, and died in Florida. I send letters to families with that name at various addresses in the Jersey Shore area, hoping that I can find a living relative. I received a phone call from one of them, and after a lengthy discussion I realize this could not have been my family. They are a close knit group and there were no hotel managers in their family history. I go on to the second pair of names.

NAME	Birth	Death	Last Residence

George Klein   2/15/1905   March 1996   Boyton Beach, FL
Issued : New Jersey

Irene Klein   4/19/1907   April 8, 1990 Boyton Beach, FL.
Issued : New Jersey

I still need to confirm this information and remove all doubt, so I call another "stranger" who has been helping me. In my searching I met a mother who gave up her child at the same time as I was adopted, used the same agency and stayed in the same home as my mother. Her name was Sally Brown and the son she gave up for adoption, I recently discovered, was a close friend of mine during my childhood. Her son's (and my childhood friend's) wife was an amateur genealogist and was ready and willing to assist me. Her experience was going to become crucial in my search. Her name was Susanne Friedman and she suggested that since we had the names of George and Irene Klein, she could look them up in the 1930 United

States census. It would give me their address in 1930, but that could serve as a starting point and I could trace them forward. Perhaps I could find the hotel they managed. Susan quickly found the data and sent it to me by E mail. How would I know that this George and Irene were really my grandparents? The truth is that I wouldn't, but each piece of information is a small piece of a puzzle.

I read the information slowly, taking in each fact; when I saw something familiar, listed in the household with George and Irene Klein was their son Marvin. When I started the search, I only knew two things about my life before I was adopted. One was the city where I was born and the other was my original name, Marvin. Who was this Marvin, it couldn't be me. I wasn't born yet. I remembered that in the narrative given to me by the adoption agency, it stated that my grandparents had a son who died of meningitis at the age of seven. It is a Jewish tradition to name children after relatives who have passed away and I must have been named after my uncle Marvin. I showed the E mail to my wife without comment and she looked at me and said, "This is your family. You were named after your uncle."

Oh my God! I am Marvin Klein, grandson of George and Irene Klein, named in honor of the tragic loss of their firstborn child. For the first time in fifty-two years I know my birth name. I know my name, Marvin Klein.

The Door of Hope

Unyielding devotion, after 52 Years,
they were ready to help me.

I was born in a home for unwed mothers run by the Salvation Army in Jersey City, New Jersey, called the Door of Hope. Today, whenever I see the Salvation Army collecting for the poor at store entrances, I have to stop and make a contribution. This American tradition has new meaning for me now. I discover that the system run by the Salvation Army is known as a Booth Home, and that I am a Booth Baby. The Salvation Army, unlike the State of New Jersey, maintains a policy of sharing information with birth mothers and their children, if I can provide them with my birth name. The Booth Homes maintain a website to enable returning children like me to contact them. There are websites with lists of Booth babies trying to find their birth parents and parents looking for the child they gave up.

I E Mail them and ask them if they have the medical records of Marvin Klein. They respond with a form and I must provide proof of my identity and a notarized signature. Seven days later a large brown envelope arrives in my mailbox from the Salvation Army. What I found in that envelope was the explanation to my powerful feelings, and to the strong connection I always felt to a mother I had never known. It would be weeks before I fully understood.

14 November, 2003
Mr Robert Hafetz
1014 Surrey Lane
Warrington, PA 18976

RE: Medical Records
Dear Mr. Hafetz;
Please find enclosed a copy of your medical records. These are being supplied to you at your request. We trust the information you are looking for is included. You will note that these records have been microfilmed so they may be difficult to read.
Please do not hesitate to contact us if we can be of any additional assistance to you.
God Bless you
In God's service

As I read through the page, the first thing I see is my mother's name, Arlene Klein. Arlene, that's my wife's first name too, only she spells it differently, Arleen. This is an interesting coincidence and I file it away in my mind. My mother's date of birth, place of birth, and address are all right there before me. The haze in my mind's eye is solidifying into a person, if only I had a picture of her. My mother is becoming real. I read the description of the Booth Home social worker as she observes the Klein's as they apply with their daughter.

10/04/50

"Mr. and Mrs. George Klein came in to make application for their daughter; Arlene. They explained that at the present time they were living at the Ambassador Hotel. Mr. and Mrs. Klein described Arlene as a capable girl. She could do almost anything. Mrs. Klein cried a little as she talked. Arlene was an only child. They would miss her so. She had been such a good girl. They didn't know how this happened."

10/25/50

"Arlene was admitted today. She is short, rather attractive young woman. One could see that the relationship between parents and daughter was a very close one. The parents seemed over solicitous. Arlene reacted as one younger than her years."

10/25/50

"I have seen Arlene frequently during this period of time. She has made a good adjustment here. Arlene experiences quite a bit of difficulty talking about the father of her baby. Since the plan for the baby is adoption, I have referred the case to Children's Home Society."

I read each word with utter amazement as I am discovering events that existed before I was born. Descriptions of my mother interacting with her parents, descriptions of my grandparents as being close and loving have an impact on me. I can't help but think of the tragedy that this family has endured; the loss of a child at age seven and now they are going to give up another child. A child named after the one they lost.

As I turn the pages, I find something I thought I would never see; something that is forever locked away from the adopted by a misguided state. There, before me, for the first time in my fifty-two years of life, is my original birth certificate. The name on it says Marvin Lee Klein. I can now say, in fact, that I am Marvin Lee Klein.

Evelyn Levine Moore

The stranger who loved me

I write once again, this time to graduates of Asbury Park High School and a woman named Evelyn writes back to me. Evelyn is the same age as my birthmother, 69, and she offers to help me in any way she can. She gives me a complete history of Jewish culture and Asbury Park, where she grew up, and describes what life was like in the '50s. She discusses my search with many of her friends; all of whom grew up in Asbury Park. They even meet me for lunch and bring their yearbooks so I can try and find a picture of someone who looks like me or one of my children. They give me the names of two Jewish girls they knew who became pregnant out of wedlock. I have discovered the gold mine of gossip, and it is a treasure trove of information. Evelyn shows me the graveyards where Jews would have been buried and she walks with me looking for a headstone of a seven-year-old boy who died in 1937. That boy would have been my uncle and finding his grave would have been a great source of information. All of their efforts didn't uncover anything specific about my family, but their commitment, support and investment in my search gave me the strength and inspiration to continue. I would soon discover part of Evelyn's strong desire to help me and the connection Evelyn had to my family.

Evelyn told me that when she was a twelve-year-old child, she ran away from home and stayed overnight in the Ambassador Hotel. The next morning when she woke up and came down to the lobby, her mother was there waiting for her and they were both overjoyed to see each other. The woman who worked behind the desk that night had the foresight to call Evelyn's mother and tell her not to worry, that her child was sleeping safe and sound in the hotel and that she would look after her. That kind, thoughtful woman was Irene Klein, my grandmother.

Cantor Ivan E. Perlman

My landsman, my friend, you carried me
when I needed you

Thanksgiving has come and gone and the days get colder and shorter. I have come so far with so little. I have learned so much, I can hardly believe what I have accomplished. The adoption agency, while helpful is very careful to protect the confidentiality of my mother. They must be discrete when approaching anyone, in order to avoid revealing the true nature of their searching. They still are mandated by law to protect the confidentiality of the birth mother. This discretion also creates a problem, how can you find who you're looking for when you can't reveal who it is. They informed me that they located a relative but refused to contact them because they are a "third party." The agency wouldn't even identify them, as that would give away the fact that they were searching for a birthmother. They would only contact the birth mother directly and inform her that the adoption agency wanted her to call them about a "very important issue." They won't even tell the natural mother that her child, now an adult, has returned and is searching for her. I knew I would have to do this myself.

I realize that I also have a responsibility to be discrete. I can't just come barging into people's lives as their child lost fifty-years years ago. How do I present myself without creating a traumatic event in their lives? They are my natural family, but the fact is, I am a stranger to them. I don't know if they know I even exist or if they have been searching for me. I have to compose a letter that identifies me as a long lost relative seeking his family. I must show them that I have enough information to convince them that I am a family member, but I can't say who I am or why I am searching. I decide that an intermediary would be a great help. Someone who could represent me, approach my family on my behalf. A Rabbi who knew them would be perfect; there would be confidentiality and trust. If I can find the synagogue which they attended, I could find a rabbi who could give me insight as to how they could best be approached.

I have compiled a list of fifteen synagogues in the Boynton Beach area that are possible candidates. I compose a letter that explains that I am a relative, separated at birth from my family, and that I believe that they were members of the synagogue. I do not say who I am looking for or that I am adopted. Jews have a strong sense of family and community. We have a saying that when you cut one Jew, we all bleed. I am depending on this closeness to work for me now.

I receive many responses that state that a review of their records didn't turn up any members with the names George and Irene Klein. One of the responses is an E mail from Cantor Ivan E. Perlman. He says if I tell him who I'm looking for and why, then he will help me. He states that he will hold my information in the strictest confidence, but I must tell him the whole truth first. I agree, and send an E mail that tells the whole story from the beginning to what I now know. Cantor Perlman writes back and states that he will help me until I find my mother and he will not rest until I am successful. He offers the help of his son in New Jersey who is a computer "wiz" and once again I have strangers devoted to helping me with no benefit to themselves. But this was not just an offer of support; this was a commitment to stick with me until the end, and he did. Little did I know just how much he will do for me, and just when I needed it.

Jill

I asked Cantor Perlman to suggest the most likely funeral homes that my family would have used for my grandparent's funeral. Funeral directors keep lists of family members who attend and are often very helpful with information. If I can locate the funeral home or cemetery, then I can get the names of family members who are very likely alive today. The Cantor gives me a list of four cemeteries and I start calling. The second call produced results; my grandparents are buried at Mount Carmel Cemetery, row 1 plots 26 and 27. The clerk informs me that the funeral home that provided the service was Riverside Gordon, of Hollywood, Florida. Everything is happening so fast; I'm moving forward by the hour, drawing ever so closer to the goal that has been so far for so long. I call Riverside Gordon and a clerk, who just started working, answers. She finds the file of George Klein and agrees to retrieve it. If I call her back in an hour, she will discuss it with me. I call her back and she is reluctant to give me any names. She's not sure about the confidentiality of the information and suspicious of me because I claim to be a grandson, but I don't know anything about my own family. After all this time I have someone on the phone that is looking at a list of my family, and won't tell me who they are. I ask if there is an Arlene Klein on the list and she says no, and there are no children on the guest list. She's very nervous, and extremely curious about the nature of the whole discussion. I find myself in a difficult position, as I can't just say I am a child born out of wedlock searching for his mother. I am very close now and the chances I will say something to the wrong person and create a scandal are increasing. After some more cat and mouse conversation, I decide to tell her the truth. I tell her that I was separated from my family at birth fifty-two years ago, I was adopted and I am trying to find any living relative. I am certain George Klein is my grandfather and that I have never seen any of my family, not even a picture. Her defenses begin to crumble, but not completely, the mother in her comes to the surface, and she gives me a name. She tells me the contact person who arranged the funeral was Gerald Safier. My first thought is why didn't my mother arrange the funeral for her parents? She won't give me the phone number, but tells me I can easily look it up. She wishes me luck and I thank her, and she asks me to call her back if I find anything. Her name is Jill.

First Contact

*How do you say hello to people who don't
know you exist*

I have the name and the phone number, but what do I say when I call? They don't know who I am or even if I exist, or perhaps they do and they have been looking for me. The hours pass as I contemplate my call, it's a cool November evening, and I am alone at work. I find a spot where I won't be disturbed and make the call. A woman answers and tells me Dr. Safier is her husband. The voice sounds like an older woman; she is interested and suspicious at the same time. She asks how I got her number and I explain that I got it from the funeral home. I tell her my name is Robert Hafetz and that I am searching for any living relatives of the Klein family, particularly Arlene Klein. I told her that I found it strange that she wasn't at her mother Irene's funeral. The woman was still somewhat confused and uncertain as to who I was and why I was asking for this information. Then she said the words that in a single moment forced a lifetime of hidden grief and fear into the open, "Arlene died many years ago and she never had any children." I was shocked! I'll never forget that moment! The words hung in the air, time stopped, my feelings were frozen, suspended, as if they could be shut down to avoid more hurt. In an instant my hopes of finding my mother and the siblings I always hoped I had were gone. At this moment I experienced a profound sense of loneliness. In a word I was lost. I told her Arlene was my mother and that I was given up for adoption. I sensed she was very upset at being the bearer of such bad news, but it wasn't her fault. Fate simply chose her, a kind, and gentle, compassionate person, to be the one to tell me. She was a good choice. I left work in a state of shock, feeling intense grief that I couldn't explain. How can I feel remorse like this for someone I had never known? It was as if my mother died this moment in the present, not many years ago. There was no funeral for me, no validation for my grief, no understanding from a world that denied adopted adults have these feelings. My wife and children love and care for me, but they do not understand how I can feel this way. All my life I had always dreamed of siblings and now that dream is gone too.   In this moment, I am truly alone. I am lost...again.

Cantor Ivan Perlman

We are never alone,

we just don't see those who are there

That evening I go to my computer to check my mail, and I see there are two Emails from Cantor Ivan Perlman. The first one says;

Date 11/16/2003

From Cantor Ivan Perlman

To Hafar1014

We had a men's club meeting this morning and I read your email to them. One woman knew George and Irene Klein and they lived in Building 5 at Village Royale on the Green at Boynton Beach. Another gentleman is going to call me with information of your family who are in California. He will give me the phone numbers and I will send them to you.

The second was dated four days later and contained the name and phone number of a man who went to the same high school as my mother.

Date 11/20/2003

From: Cantor Ivan Perlman

To: Hafar1014

Tonight call AL STEPNER

He went to school with your mother and is related to cousins. He can tell you everything.

My long shot was paying off, who would think a man I found on the net would know someone, who knew someone else, who went to high school with my birthmother? Community is a beautiful thing. We are never alone; we just don't see those that are there.

Big Al Stepner

We all have a Big Al in our lives

I call Al Stepner, who tells me he went to high school with my mother. Al, known as Big Al, was the president of the home owner's association where my grandparents lived in Boynton Beach. Al is a warm and friendly kind of guy, someone you feel like you've known all your life when you meet him for the first time. Al feels like family to me and his casual warmth and kindness fill me with strength. Al went to high school with my mother and he tells me as much as he can about her as a teen. He also lived in the same retirement community as my grandparents and he knew them very well. Al gives me a phone number and tells me this is my cousin Pat Lewis and she was very close to Arlene. "Call her and talk to her, tell her Big Al Stepner sent you". I haven't come this far to give up and I will learn what I can about my family. Big Al has given me far more than a phone number, he has given me hope and the belief that my search isn't over.

Knowledge of the death of my mother and the absence of any siblings denies me resolution. I had always defined home and belonging as finding acceptance from them and now they could never be found.

Pat Lewis

The moment every adopted person dreams of

Every adopted adult who searches dreams of the moment when he finds his home once again. Home is not a place, but a feeling of love, belonging, and acceptance by the natural family. It is a moment of great personal validation for us; to reunite, by a willful act, with the security that was taken from us and use that validation experience to resolve the grief we feel all our lives.

I dial the number of Pat Lewis. "Hello, my name is Robert Hafetz and Big Al Stepner gave me your number." Pat was confused and, at first, thought I was Al Stepner. My mind struggles with the situation, and I wonder how can I convince someone as to who I am, when they have no idea I ever existed. In my mind I become the child whose destiny was never realized, I became Marvin. I will speak to Pat Lewis as her cousin Marvin Klein. I continue, "When I was born I was given another name, it was Marvin Lee Klein, Arlene Klein was my mother." The line becomes silent. She is confused and has no idea who I am. After a long pause Pat proclaims, "Arlene only had three sons and you can't be one of them." Oh my God, I have three brothers! The intense grief resulting from knowledge of the death of my mother begins to melt away as I discover the existence of my brothers. I continue, "I am the first born son of Arlene Klein, George and Irene Klein were my grandparents. I was given up for adoption." I hear a gasp and then Pat says, "We always suspected, but we were never certain. Wait!" She puts me on the speaker phone and calls her entire family to the phone so I can tell them the story all at once. I hear them all talking at the same time, and in the background I hear a man trying to get a word in, but it's hopeless. I hear a doorbell ring over the phone and I hear voices call them over to the phone. There's a lot of talking, and shushing before they settle down. I tell them the whole story starting with the past eight months and ending at the present moment. They welcome me, they accept me; they make me feel like I belong among them. This is the moment I have been searching for. Pat tells me wonderful things about my mother and says; "Arlene would have been thrilled to see you again." I have returned home.

In the weeks that followed, my cousin, Pat, described my mother's personality to me. I still didn't have a picture of my mother, but I was creating a memory of what she was, loving, generous, attractive, and she held the family together. In the weeks that follow, I learn that only two people were aware that I existed, Pat's sister, Elaine Bennett, and my mother's close friend Penny Price. Pat mails me a family tree that describes one hundred and fifty years of history, and there's more, pictures of my mother and her family. As I look at my mother's picture for the first time, I am struck by the strong resemblance to my wife. The resemblance is so striking that when I show the picture to my wife's family and ask them who they think it is, they all respond, it's Arleen, your wife. Is this a coincidence or is it indication of something more, an unconscious memory, or a suppressed emotion finding its way to the surface? When I was an infant, I saw my mother's face, and heard her name spoken, but since I couldn't speak or think in words I had no conscious memory of her. I had emotions, the emotions of an infant bonded to his mother, and in those emotions the memories of her face and her name were living in me. They are not replaced by the love of my wonderful adopted family, and they did not fade as the decades passed, in fact they became stronger, compelling me to make life choices in relationships, education, and my careers. The sensations and images of my mother were not remembered, and never forgotten.

I describe my family here in the hope that one of their descendants will someday read a name they recognize in this book.

I am a descendent of Leopold Fuchs (1855-1924) and his wife Mathilda Lapper 1855- 1935) who were married in Wesritz, Austria in 1881. They had six children; Max, Pauline, Sam, Richard, Alex, and Olga. Pauline was my great grandmother and she married Max Seidal on March 27, 1904. They had two children Mildred and Irene. Irene married George Klein on Jan 5, 1905, and had two children, Marvin and Arlene. Marvin died at the age of seven and Arlene was my mother. Arlene gave birth to me on January 28, 1951. Arlene married Herbert Glasser on November 15,

1952. They had three sons, Dennis, Marc, and Keith. Mildred married Sam Levy on October 30, 1932 and had two children, Patricia and Elaine. Patricia is Pat, my cousin. I, Robert Hafetz, married Arleen Tatz on July 15, 1973 and we have three children, Jessica, Danielle, and Matthew. To me, the words resound like a prayer, and the knowledge of what they represent has the power to validate my path in life. If words can heal, then let these words be my medicine. I am lost, no more.

Pat tells me that my natural mother's husband lives in Texas and that I should try and contact him. Talking to the man who married my birth mother would give me the crucial insight as to what she was really like, but contacting him could be a very delicate issue. I don't know how my intrusion upon his life will be received. He could see me as a connection to his wife or as a bad memory becoming real. He may wonder why after so long I am approaching him now. He may not even know I exist. Whatever I do, the result is going to be a shock to his emotions. After much contemplation I decide writing a letter will be the least traumatic way to introduce myself. I compose a letter that stresses the wonderful life I had, and that I hold no resentment to anyone regarding my adoption. I want to convey to him that I am a well adjusted, happy, well cared for person who longs to know the truth about his mother, and her family. I want to convey the sense of loss I have to someone who has lost the same person. I lost my mother in my infancy and he lost her to death. We share the same sense of grief over the loss of the same person. I am hoping he will see me in that light and reach out to me as I reach out to him.

Two weeks later I receive a letter from Bolch Spring, Texas. It is written by Phyllis Glasser, Herb's second wife. Phyllis tells me that Herb is still in a state of shock over receiving my letter and that she will speak to me on his behalf. Phyllis offers to help and she commits herself to helping me learn as much as possible about my mother and her family. Phyllis has embraced me as if I were a member of her family, and has told me that I may consider myself as such. To those of us whose emotions have been abandoned in the system of adoption, belonging is everything. Again, a stranger has offered to help, and again, I am reminded of the innate goodness of so many human beings. I bring obligation and uncertainty into their lives and she responds to me with her outstretched arms and warmth. Later Phyllis tells me that as a child, she gave up her baby to be adopted. Phyllis has always been a member of my family of circumstance. After meeting me she is going to renew her search for him. She placed a contact letter with the adoption agency so that if he should ever return, he would be able to find her. I may have made a difference in the life of someone I don't know.

The Monkey Bank

A message across time

When I call Phyllis on the phone, I always hear Herb in the background actively involved in the conversation, giving advice and suggestions, playing an important role, but still distant. I ask for pictures and something more, I want to touch something my mother touched, hold something she held. I want something real that she had a connection to. Phyllis tells me that Arlene was a serious artist and worked with ceramics and mosaic tiles. She made a ceramic monkey bank a few years ago and she would ask Herb if I could have it. Herb agreed and soon the bank was on its way to me.

A week later a small package, the size of a half gallon carton of milk, arrives. I see by the return address it's from Phyllis and Herb Glasser, so I know it's something from my mother. As I open the box, the events of the past year flash by my mind: the dead ends, the breakthroughs, the people who helped me, the moments of triumph and the periods of frustration.

The fear I felt when I called Pat Lewis and the first sense of returning home when her family embraced me. A life of simmering grief began to leave me in that moment and the healing process started in earnest. That moment was pure magic and this moment was approaching that one, as I was about to hold an object made by my birth mother. Not just any object, but an object of art made by her. All art consists of two virtues; there is first the technique, and then the meaning that makes it unique. I am about to touch an essence of what she was through the art she created. I remove a shape encased in a more than adequate amount of bubble wrap. It's a brown ceramic monkey, but there is something about it that...My God!... it's a baby. It's clearly a baby sitting peacefully with a look of contentment on its face. As I cradle it in my hands, I can't help but wonder, did my mother think of the baby she gave up for adoption while she was making it? I'm sure my mother never imagined that it would travel across half the country, arriving thirty years later in the hands of that very child. When she made this, I'm certain she thought of me and now that I hold it, I am thinking of her. In this moment we are connected by this object, from her hands to mine across a lifetime.

My Brothers

An adopted child's dream becomes true

Eighteen months after my adoption my natural mother married and had three sons, Keith, Marc, and Dennis Glasser. I am thrilled beyond words to have brothers. Adopted adults I have spoken to all report that they dream of brothers and sisters waiting to be found. In my adopted family, I was an only child and I daydreamed often of siblings. Now I have found them. Unfortunately, Dennis died from heart disease at the age of forty-two, leaving two children, Alicia, Corwin and his wife Linda. Keith lives just outside of Dallas, has no children, and Marc who is divorced, lives in Florida. Marc has two children. Phyllis asks me if I would give my permission for her to tell Keith that he has a brother, and I agree. She gives me his Email and screen name so I can contact him by instant messaging. That night at 11:00 PM, I go online and sure enough there he is, my brother. I stare at the screen in disbelief, my brother Keith, is right there in

89

front of me. Never in my wildest dreams did I imagine that my first contact with my brother would be on a computer. I type "Hey Keith", and he replies "Hey." He knows who I am, Phyllis told him about me. We talk about nothing for an hour, and it doesn't matter, he's my brother.

A few days later Phyllis asks me if she can tell Marc about me and I enthusiastically agree. Marc calls me the next day and he can't stop talking. He is excited to have a new brother, and over the next few weeks he tells me everything I could ever think to ask about our mother. Her love of art, and her talent as an artist, her kindness, and that she was the glue that held the family together. He tells me in detail about their life in Irvington, New Jersey, and their move to Texas. Marc calls me often and he reaches out to me in order to draw me closer to him. I accept, after all he's my brother.

The Trip to Texas to Meet Herb, Phyllis, and Keith

It was to be a magic moment

It is a warm June night as my wife and I arrive in Dallas International Airport. I am approaching the end of my search, which started one and one half years ago on a cold February night. After meeting Herb and Phyllis, my wife and I will drive to Houston to meet Penny Price, my mother's closest friend. Penny will take us to the cemetery where I will stand before my mother's grave and seek to find closure after fifty-three years apart.

At 6:00 the next morning my cell phone rings and its Herb making arrangements to meet. Herb never called me before, so I'm surprised that's he's calling me now. It has always been Phyllis who called me with Herb in the background. He may be feeling more comfortable with me and is closing the distance between us. At 7:30 they arrive at our hotel, Herb, Phyllis, Keith, and Marylyn, Keith's wife. We recognized one another at first glance, and after formal introductions, we had breakfast. We sat down together and I sat next to my brother Keith. Herb looked somewhat tense and unsure of the situation. Then suddenly Herb stood up, took over, and changed everyone's seat so he could sit next to me. Then everyone faded into the background and it was only Herb and I at the table. He brought a shopping bag full of family albums and proceeded to explain every person in each picture to me. It was a wonderful history lesson, everything I ever wanted to know and here were the answers. Herb went to great lengths to explain his side of the family to me as well as my mother's side. This is a man who never said two words to me and suddenly he was warm friendly and talking up a storm. Something changed in him I don't know what but I'm glad for it. He asked me if I ever found my father and then he asked what month I was born in. At the end of breakfast, Herb said "Goodbye son." Then asked, "What should I call you, my step son once removed?" He didn't want to leave and neither did I. We eventually shook hands and left. My wife and I started the long drive to Houston.

Penny and Mickey Price

Sometimes friends are closer than family

After a four hour drive to Houston, my wife and I arranged to meet the next morning with Penny and her husband Mickey Price. Penny is Herb's cousin. The Prices and the Glassers maintained a very close friendship for many years. In Irvington, they lived in close proximity to each other, socializing on a regular basis. In the late '50s early '60s, Irvington and the Jersey Shore area were in a state of economic decline and many residents moved to other parts of the country for a better opportunity. Houston, Texas, with its growing oil industry, was the chosen destination of my birthmother's family. Penny and Mickey motivated by the same economic needs, but also wanting to keep their close relationship intact went along with them. Penny was one of only three people who knew I existed. Herb knew and Elaine, a cousin in Florida, also knew. My birth mother didn't discuss any details with Herb saying only that she gave away a baby for adoption. Few details about my adoption were ever mentioned to anyone, but Arlene did say she intended to search for me someday. For the most part she buried her feelings just as I did. If only I could have known, I would have searched for her sooner. Penny and I had spoken on the phone a few times and she was able to, through her eyes, portray my mother for me. We had become close and I know my presence brought her old sorrow back to the surface. I was a connection to someone she loved dearly and it was hard on her feelings. Nevertheless, Penny offered to take me to my natural mother's gravesite if I was ever in Texas.

We agreed to meet for breakfast and get acquainted before traveling to the cemetery. I felt an immediate attachment to these kind hearted people. I could see in their faces that meeting me had aroused their feelings of grief over the loss of their friend Arlene. They described my natural mother as warm, loving and hard working. She was an artist and felt very passionate about life. She painted, and worked with pottery and mosaic tiles. Mickey wept openly as he described the events leading up to my mother's death and her last moments of life. Having a history of congestive heart failure, my natural mother was hospitalized for pneumonia. Mickey believed her doctor discharged her too early. Within a week, my natural mother suffered heart failure in the middle of the night and never recovered.

After breakfast we followed Penny and Mickey to the cemetery. We entered along a road bordered by trees on each side. I felt like I was entering a park rather than a cemetery. Penny lead the way and after searching for a few minutes we found ourselves standing side by side before a modest plaque in the grass. She moved closer to me placing her arm around me. I needed her support and I believe she needed mine as well. It was quiet, so quiet. We were locked in the moment together, the three of us.

It was my desire to find my mother alive that drove me never to surrender to hopelessness. However, as fate would have it, this was a destiny not meant for me. My search began nine months before and ended beside a grave in Bellaire, Texas. There were no headstones in this place. It appeared as a gentle meadow, not a place of the departed. There were trees with red blossoms casting shadows on the grass as if watching lovingly over the souls with whom they shared their world. The graves were all marked by small plaques lying on the grass. As I knelt beside hers, the words Arlene Hope Glasser gazed up at me. I remember thinking Hope, her name is Hope. We are together again, the circle is closed.

Why I Chose to Search

I once cared for a client who had Cerebral Palsy. She was confined to a wheelchair, her arms and legs were locked in, immovable; she was dependent on others for her every need, and yet she was genuinely happy. I remember another client who suffered from Multiple Sclerosis. Before the onset of her disease, she experienced a far higher level of ability and self determination; she was confined to a wheelchair for a limited time, had periods of remission, and yet was extremely angry and bitter. How can this be, when the one with the profoundly greater disability was happy, and the one with the less severe disability was chronically angry? The answer can be found in one word, loss. The young woman with Cerebral Palsy was born as she now is and never experienced the loss of her ability, while the woman with MS once could walk, talk, and live, like anyone else, but lost those abilities. An adopted adult once had the bond of a mother and lost it. How then does one explain this loss to another who has not experienced it? Physical loss is apparent to all who observe, but emotional loss is much more difficult to convey. Further, how does an adopted adult explain the emotional loss so profoundly felt, when he can't comprehend it himself? It was fifty-three years before I could put a word to the sense of loss I have been feeling all my life. That word was grief. When asked, today, I can say that I feel a profound sense of grief for the mother who carried me and gave birth to me. We all know what grief is, but then how can I explain the grief I feel for someone I knew before I could speak or think. The answer to that question lies in the heart of every woman who gave birth to a child and the emotion she felt for that newborn child. During those first days of life, does the newborn a mother cradles in her arms know how much he is loved by her? Perhaps the answer lies in the words I use. The infant doesn't know, the infant feels and remembers. I did and, I still do.

I experienced a profound loss as an infant, before I could speak or think. How then do I come to resolve powerful emotions that call to me for healing? It's as if they speak a unique language, get stronger with the years, and come to the surface of my mind when they sense my weakness in blocking them. They are always there, relentless, and unyielding, always demanding my attention; asserting itself in my everyday life, silently, forging my personality, and guiding my life's choices.

During the last ten years of my life, I have worked in the adult and adolescent mental health system as an adjunctive therapist. As part of the treatment team, I have counseled many adults and children in dealing with their sense of loss, grief and trauma. In many cases the process had very similar components, first, recognition of the loss by another human being, second, a journey, returning to the original moment of the grief, if possible. Not literally, but a journey, but figuratively speaking, an odyssey of the soul, to re-experience the feeling in an attempt to better understand it. To see it clearly and bring it forth so it can be understood not feared. Understanding is the antidote to fear and grief. Remorse, acceptance, and then peace, hopefully will follow.

When one experiences a profound loss, there is a need to regain that which was lost, and to make whole that which is now in part. It's simple to understand a material loss, but a spiritual loss, a loss of the self, is more difficult to explain. For me, the adopted adult, the method was the search for my history, to know my name, my mother's face, my family history, and the events that caused my mother to release me to a life without her. As a result of this search, I found validation, in the help and compassion from strangers I encountered, a conscious awareness of my grief, an understanding why it happened, who I was, and ultimately, closure.

My Two Mothers

My adoption was arranged before I was born and should have gone smoothly after my birth, but my natural mother refused to sign the release for adoption. For five months, she delayed the adoption as she sought a way to keep me. It must be difficult for a seventeen-year-old child to resist the pressure from the Adoption agency, her parents, and adoptive family, all demanding that she go through with the adoption as arranged. While my mother resisted the process, I lived in a foster home, visited often by my natural mother. During those five months the bonding of mother and child intensified. My mother named me after her departed brother, most likely, to compel her parents to keep me themselves. I believe my maternal grandmother, Irene, also saw me as a replacement for her son, Marvin, who died at the age of seven. It must have been terribly painful for her as well as for my mother.

I am a blessing and a scandal all at the same time. The adoption agency told me that there was some serious discussion between my grandparents as they considered adopting me themselves. It was not to be and eventually my mother gave in and I became the child of Dr. Morris and Florence Hafetz. After my adoption was final, my natural mother wrote frequently to the agency asking for information about how I was doing in my new home. The letters continued for two years and then simply stopped. Clearly my natural mother wasn't letting me go so easily. In speaking to her cousin, Elaine Bennett, I discovered that she always intended to come back for me.

My adopted mother Florence was all too aware of this and it filled her with a fear that she carried for the rest of her life. When I was a child, she never spoke of my adoption and even as an adult when I would ask; she would refuse to discuss it. I could see the pain on her face and, out of loyalty and love for her, I could never press the issue. The issue, however, never stopped pressing me. Florence always felt she should share what she knew with me, but her fear kept her from doing it.

My natural mother, although unseen, was a real part of the relationship between adopted child and adopted mother. As a child I could never understand the emotions Florence was feeling, but today, as an adult I understand them all too well. She was fearful that no matter how much she loved me, I would always have a longing for my natural mother, who fought the adoption and wrote letters to my adopted family for two years. The possibility that our mother-child relationship could be shared was too terrible for Florence to imagine. It was one thing for her to resist the ghost of my natural mother, but when I asked it became even more threatening. The prevailing wisdom of the era was that the adopted child will have no memory of his natural mother and consequently no desire to know anything about her. Just as I suppressed my grief, my mother suppressed her fear. There it was between us, unmentioned, and yet profoundly felt by us both. Somewhere else a young woman was suppressing her grief too.

Like most fears they are larger in thought, than in actuality. There has never been any question in my mind as to who my mother was. She was the woman who nurtured me, raised me, supported me, and guided me for fifty years. I cannot however forget the mother who I was part of, and who gave birth to me. The mother, who fought for me and after much pressure, lost me in the adoption process. She believed that no matter how much she loved me it was best for me to be adopted. One does not replace or displace the other; they both are a part of me and me of them.

Florence Hafetz

Arlene Klein

My Father

Questions, questions,

my life,

is full of questions.

The creation of a new life always involves three people, mother, child, and a father. Due to the symbiotic nature of the mother-child relationship, the bonding process begins before birth and continues to strengthen immediately after birth. The bonding process with the father comes later in the child's life or in my case never. Consequently, the desire to know the identity of my father is less compelling than the need to know my mother, but important none the less. In my case the search for my birth mother has ended in a cemetery. Because of this, the only hope I have of finding one of my birth parents alive rests in finding my father.

My birth mother named a man as my father in the adoption agency record. Even with his name and a description of his family, I have, as of this writing, been unable to find him. I have discovered a family that fits the description in the record, and traced their history in great detail. Using the census of Great Britain I discovered their home address in Cardiff, Wales in 1902. I also found their names on the ship's manifest of the Mauritania, when they immigrated to America in 1919. They were married the same year. I found them again listed on the passenger list of the Berengaria, in 1924, as they traveled to Wales, had a baby, and returned to America the same year. I discovered their home address in Summit, New Jersey and then their move to New Providence, New Jersey. I found them listed in the New Providence city directory in 1929. The adoption agency record stated that my paternal grandfather worked in a parking lot, while the city directory said he managed a parking garage. That's not exact but it's a good match. Their ages as stated in the record also match so I am convinced this is the right family. I trace their entire lives from their births to their deaths, almost a century later. When I read the summary of their lives I have compiled, I can't help but think how their time flows through my hands like sand.

The trail leads me to an upscale, women's clothing store in New Providence called the Janette Shop. I am searching for someone who knew my suspected paternal grandmother. I speak to the daughter of the store's original owner and she remembers the person I am searching for. After a few minutes of conversation, I realize that this cannot be the family listed in the record. The descriptions don't match, she is a young widow, and she only had two children. The record says she never worked but she was employed in this store. One of her sons died young in a farm accident and the other's whereabouts are not known to her. This cannot be the family my birth mother described but there are too many connections to be just by chance. The Janette Shop is only a short drive from my mother's home in Irvington, New Jersey, and her mother Irene, was involved in upscale women's clothes. It's very likely that they all knew each other with the common link, women's clothes. I believe that the woman who worked for the Janette Shop was the model for a carefully crafted family that was never real.

The social worker at the adoption agency told me that often the expectant mother would make up a fictitious name to protect the identity of the real father. If my birth mother lied to protect the real father then I can assume that she loved him very much. Then why didn't they get married and keep me? 1950 was a different age with different values. It isn't likely that a sixteen-year-old girl, pregnant by a twenty-one-year-old year old man, would have been accepted by the family or the community. It was also a crime. Adoption allows my family to keep my existence a secret. The false name for my father protects the real father from prosecution and reprisal from her family. George Klein was known as a tough guy and he would not have been happy about his child becoming pregnant. My mother could continue her relationship with the real birthfather, only if his identity was kept from her father. Did my mother have to choose between her baby and the man she loved? Did she believe that she could return for me as my adopted mother feared? Did Irene Klein, my grandmother, see me as a replacement for her son Marvin who passed away at the tender age of seven? What toll did this take on her emotions? In life there will always be mystery and mine has more than its share. For every mystery solved another comes to the fore.

For my father, should he ever read this, I am grateful to you for choosing the woman from which I have come, for being part of that which makes me what I am. You were both there when I chose the woman who is now my wife and you are both here as I write this memoir. From you, I have given a gift to humanity, my three children, your grandchildren. Without you they could not have come into being. What happened in that moment between two children so long ago, the moment in which I was created, was a blessing, not a scandal. To you I will always feel gratitude and love. I am grateful that I am, and that you were.

In Conclusion

Was it worth it?

I have spent nine months of countless hours and sleepless nights staring at a computer screen. There were periods of hope followed by periods of hopelessness. I made long trips to strange cities, spending hours in libraries examining old documents that spanned over half a century. I felt as if I was riding an emotional roller coaster, experiencing a lifetime of failures in less than a year. Considering all the time involved and my emotional investment, all of my efforts brought me to a grave in Texas. I must pause and ask myself, was it worth it? What do I have to show for all of that? A name, a face, my history, two living brothers, cousins, knowledge that I was loved, wanted and not given up easily, words to describe the emotions I feel, and a path for my grief to leave the place in my heart where it has dwelled for 53 years. I heard my inner voice, but I never understood it until now. I wanted answers to the core questions that determine who one really is. Who were the people who created me and who created them? Why was I cast away, with no will of my own, to share the destiny of two strangers? I already had a mother, but she set me free. I am not just alone I am lost, and one needs to be found, when one is lost. My search is a journey of self-exploration. It is my journey to find myself. For most of my life, my heart remembered but my mind could not see it. Grief demands a resolution that can begin only when the mind becomes aware of it. The prize at the end of this marathon is knowledge, dignity, peace of mind, and a monkey bank that sits on my desk. Was it worth it? I never looked back; I never doubted it. Now, at the end of my search I know I would do it again in a heartbeat.

I wrote this book for everyone, not just those who are members of the adoption family. For those of you not part of the adoption family, I hope you have a greater understanding of us. It is my hope that by sharing my experience, I can help those whose lives have been changed by adoption. I want to provide a guide for them that will enable the exploration of their past emotions. The journey into one's self is the most difficult and most rewarding voyage one will ever embark upon. The purpose of which is to rediscover that which has always been ours.

"Though the earth and all inferior creatures be common to all men, yet every man has a property in his own person; this nobody has a right to but himself."

John Locke

(1690)

A Letter to My Natural Mother

April 2, 2005

Dear Birth Mother, Arlene Klein

I write to you now because it's the only way I can express my feelings to you. All my life I have wondered what you looked like, what your name was, and why you let me go. Did you love me or was I just an inconvenience, or a problem? I didn't ask to be, but I came into your world and you sent me away from it. You left me with powerful memories I couldn't understand or explain. Memories that I buried deep in my unconscious yet demanded to be known; memories that spoke to me in the language of emotions such as fear, loneliness, worthlessness, and abandonment. For years I pretended they didn't exist, denying them when asked if I ever wondered about my adoption. When I try to open the door to those feelings, all I see is fire and blinding light. I am overwhelmed and frightened

115

by their intensity, yet I know that once the door is opened it can never be closed again. So I keep my emotions locked away, and out of sight, but they are not out of mind. They thrive and grow, increasing in intensity. They are there when I make a friend, fall in love and lose a friend. They cast a light in my heart that shows the great emptiness within. I fight to keep them buried and they fight to come out but I don't understand how to talk to them, or explain them to others. These emotions were forged before I could speak or think so I don't have words for them. How do I make others understand? Only you will understand, and in knowing who you were I will then understand. I need to see your face, hear your voice, and feel your warmth once again. I must return to the moment when I was ripped away from you, and understand with my adult mind why it happened. Only then, with knowledge, can I overcome my fears.

Now that I have found you, mother, I am at peace. I can call you by your name, I can see a picture of your face, I have the memories of those who loved you and knew you. I can hold in my hands something you created with your own. The fire has diminished to a warm glow and the bright light is now a glimmer. The emotions that frightened me now comfort me only because I know the truth. I am glad you were and that I am. I hope you are proud of me.

With love from your son

Robert Hafetz/Marvin Klein

Picture of the Monkey Bank